————————→

* **Values** are the principles by which a person lives.
They are abstract concepts that determine our behavior.

Acceptance
Benevolence
Braveness
Commitment
Communication
Consistency
Empathy
Faith
Family
Forgiveness
Frankness
Freedom
Freshness
Friendship
Gratitude
Honesty
Hope
Humility
Humor
Impartiality
Independence
Integrity
Judiciousness
Justice
Kindness
Love
Loyalty
Optimism
Patience
Peace
Punctuality
Respect
Responsibility
Self-improvement
Selflessness
Sensitivity
Serenity
Simplicity
Sociability
Solidarity
Sympathy
Tolerance
Understanding
...

I am...

```
drawing/picture
```

and my **values*** are:

_____

_____

_____

_____

_____

From Stress to
SELF-BEING

Lucía Toro

A genuine revolution for your mind.

Index

BIOGRAPHY - AUTHOR

Hiii!!! I'm Lucía Toro, daughter of Ramón Toro and Loli Márquez from Santaella, Córdoba (Spain) When i was a child I enjoyed playing and building cabins, I dreamed about becoming an architect.

In 2009, I got my degree in Architecture in the University of Granada, Spain. I specialized in Interior Design and in Project Management in the University of Seville, Spain. I also studied Graphic Design, Marketing, Advertising, Staging and Furniture to complement my degrees.

For years, I've been working on the interior design industry, conducting projects really interesting and satisfactory, professionally speaking.

But it was in 2017, after being hurt in an accident, when BOOOOOOOM...
...in a split second, I was laying in bed and almost unable to move.

Laying there, "doing nothing" caused me more stress, and that is because we live in a society that is getting more demanding by the minute.

There is an Arab proverb that says: "Books, paths, and days make a man wise."

I got my degree as a Personal Coach in the University of Málaga, Spain.

**I understood that everything happens for a reason
and that happiness lies within oneself.**

With this manual, I am trying to help you cope with stressful situations so you can go with the flow in life and show your real BEING.

All my love,

pfff...

Introduction

pfff...

...DO!!

All human beings look for happiness. But happiness cannot be found outside, it lies within everyone of us.

Having a keen understanding of our values, focusing on the present, loving ourselves unconditionally and being thankful are key elements to be happy.

So... What happens?

Our **mind** "betrays" us.

Just think about anything but a panda bear.

What did you think about? Haha... I believe it was a panda bear. Why didn't you think about a giraffe, a house, a child, a tree,...?

That is how our mind works: it mocks you, it gets distracted, it is obsessive, unstable, unsatisfied, confused, reactive, excessive, playful, fibber... But, at its core, it is calm and clear, without conditioning.

We have to calm it down and tame it so it can be out ally in life.

"Wind brings clouds and wind itself makes them vanish again, mind forges slavery and it is also mind itself that forges freedom."

Shankaracharya

pfff…

Instructions

The Stone

(translation of a poem by Antonio Pereira)

The distracted one, tripped on it.
The violent one, used it as a projectile.
The enterprising one, built with it.
The tired walker, used it as a seat.
It served as a toy for children.
Drummond wrote poetry about it.
David killed Goliath.
Michelangelo created the most beautiful sculpture out of it.

And in every single case,
the difference was not in the stone, but in the man.

Remember...
There is no stone in your path that you cannot take advantage
of in order to grow.

pfff...

...DO!!

As our mind is a little twerp... Let's keep it simple.

We start out with information.
"Stress": What is it? Its stages, its symptoms, its sources and perception.

We keep with our strategy: **pfff... + ...DO!!!**

There is a "stone" (stressful situation) in your path (life).

Pfff...: Exercises to pause your mind. You can do whichever you prefer.

...DO!!!: Decode + Operate

Exercises to asses the "stone" (stressful situation) and identify the twisting made by your mind.

Exercises to provide other options to our mind and keep walking along the path (life).

Before, during or after this, you can be **Thankful** and use the **Blank pages** to do whatever you want.

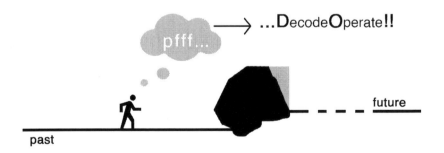

pfff...

...DO!!

Stress

...sign that means you have lost <u>the present.</u>

pfff…

WHAT IS IT?

The term "stress" (from the Latin, stringere, tighten) seems to be known by everyone, but it is really hard to define it accurately.

- Stress is every stimulus susceptible to triggers a Fight-or-flight response. (Cannon, 1929)

- Stress is the nonspecific response of the body to any demand imposed upon it. (Selye, 1974)

- Stress is every process, originated outside or inside a person, that impose some kind of urgency or request on the organism, which resolution or management requires the effort or activity of the psychic system, before any other system is activated or involved. (Engel, 1962)

- Stress is a particular relationship between the person and the environment that is appraised by the person as taxing or exceeding his or her resources and endangering his or her well-being. (Lazarus, 1984)

We can say stress is the response process generated when a person perceives a situation as a threat.

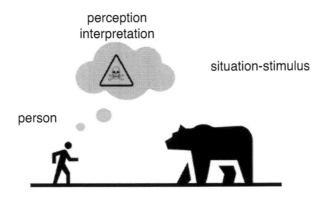

THE STAGES

The response to a threatening situation has three stages, described by Hans Selye (1950).

Stages of the General Adaptation Syndrome

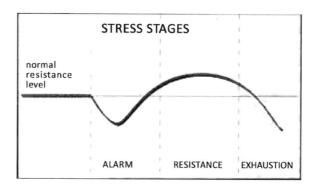

1. Alarm Stage

When facing a threat, our body responses automatically releasing adrenaline into different parts of it to provide us a fast boost so we can fight or flee.

Our breathing, pulse rate and heartbeat speed up so the muscles can respond faster. Our pupils dilate and blood flows faster and away from the digestive system to avoid vomit. Attention and concentration increase.

This stage is brief and it is not harmful if there is time to recover from it.

...DO!!

2. Resistance Stage

When the alarm stage repeats itself or goes on for a while, our body reacts adapting to the required effort.

If there is nothing it can do to go back to the original organic balance, an overburden appears that affects our performance.

Intermittent headaches, chronic fatigue, circulatory issues, heavy legs, muscle contractions in neck, upper back and lower back, brief memory loss, stomachache, nervous tics, sleep disorders, lack of focus, pessimism...

3. Exhaustion Stage

When our body cannot maintain that effort, after that continued resistance, it runs out of energy, our inner balance breaks, our immune system gets affected, our capacity to resist pathogenic agents of any kind decreases and illness appears.

SYMPTOMS

Stress may cause different symptoms: physical, emotional, cognitive and behavioral ones.

Physical symptoms

- Headache
- Diarrhea or constipation
- Nausea and dizziness
- Chest peain
- Fast palpitations
- Decrease of sexual appetite
- Breathing difficulties

Emotional symptoms

- Mood swings
- Irritability
- Nervousness, anxiety
- Overwhelming feeling
- Loneliness, isolation
- Depression
- Apathy

Cognitive symptoms

- Memory loss
- Lack of focus
- Vague discernment
- Negativity
- Constant concern
- Unhealthy thoughts
- Confusion

Behavioral symptoms

- Impulsiveness
- Aggressiveness
- Excess
- Addictions
- Nervous habits (tics, scratching, touching, biting...)
- Freeze up, mental blocks, running away

...DO!!

SOURCES

Stress may be triggered by:

- **External stimuli:** financial problems, family problems, work over-
  load, fear, the loss of a loved one, of a job, move to another place,
  a divorce, etc...

- **Inner stimuli of a person (psycho-physical):** negative thinking,
  inferiority feelings, sociological problems, intense pain, illness, etc...

PERCEPTION

Perception is the process of organize and understand the stimuli received.

It is the **mental image** you create with the help of your experiences and
needs.

pfff...

...DO!!

pfff...

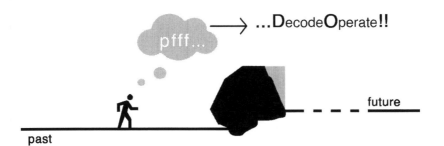

...DecodeOperate!!

pfff...

future

past

pfff...

pfff...

 —— According to Wiktionary, it is an expression of annoyance or disappointment.

It is also used to express tiredness.

When our body detects a "threat" (a real or an imaginary one), that automatically triggers some physiological responses to proceed to the basic and adaptive Fight-or-flight response.
The problem is that, when we are constantly stressed out, those responses are not adaptive and we can start feeling pain in our chest, a tingling sensation in our limbs, a suffocating feeling, tension, shivers, etc...

Before that happens, you are going to say **pfff... exhaling the "f" through your mouth.** Breathe out all the air inside you to connect with the present moment, the only thing that exists. The longer you can keep the exhalation the better.

After that, make some exercise to recover control over your attention. Without any criticism* and patiently, ok?? Just choose **BEING and...**

. **Breathe**

. **Stretch**

. **Observe**

. **Draw**

. **Imagine**

* It is normal that some thoughts come to your mind. Do not fight them back, accept them calmly and get back to focus on the exercise. It is also normal to lose track of your breathing. It is okay, just start counting again.

pfff...

 · **Breathe**

...in a controlled way to activate your vagus nerve, which goes from the base of your brain to the abdomen, and is responsible for the responses of the autonomic nervous system. Lower your heart rate and you blood pressure, treat yourself to calm.

Breathe

...with the deepest sea

- Take a deep breath through your nose.
- Hold the air inside for three seconds. (1) (2) (3)
- Breathe out completely through your nose.

Repeat 5 times.

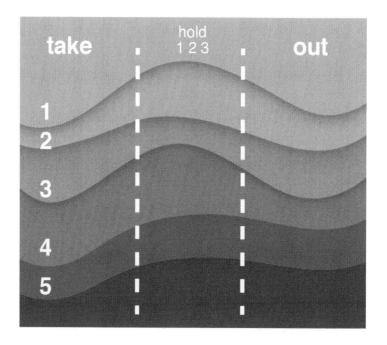

Breathe

...with the elevators

Close your right nostril with your thumb and breathe in only through the left nostril.

When you reach the inhalation limit, put your thumb away from the right nostril and close the left one with your ring finger. Breathe out.

Complete the cycle, alternating the nostrils.

Repeat 5 times.

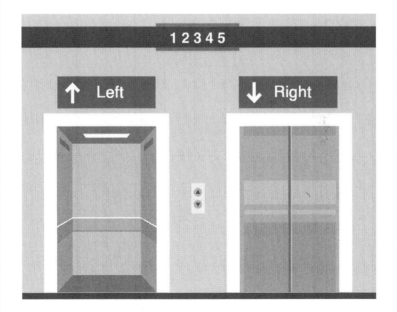

Breathe

... with the balloons

Put one hand on your abdomen and the other one on your chest.

Now, take a deep breath through your nose. You must feel how your abdomen inflates (the diaphragm gets lower and fills our belly because of the pressure applied).

Hold the air for a few seconds and breath out loudly through your mouth.

Repeat 5 times.

Breathe

... with the paintings

- Breath in for 4 seconds.
- Hold the air for 4 seconds.
- Breath out for 4 seconds.
- Do not breath in again for 4 seconds.

Repeat 5 times.

pfff...

...DO‼

· Loosen up

...the muscle tension of your body. Lower your cortisol levels and release endorphins (the hormones of happiness), increase your well-being feeling.

Loosen up

... the face

Tighten (*) for 10 seconds and relax for 30 seconds.

(*)

1°- Your forehead
2°- Your eyes
3°- Your teeth

... the neck

Tighten it for 10 seconds and relax.

Repeat 3 times.

Loosen up

... the hands

Clench your fists for 10 seconds and relax.

Repeat 3-5 times.

... the shoulders

Keep your shoulders up for 10 seconds and relax.

Repeat 3-5 times.

pfff…

 · Observe

... with the highest of attentions. Avoid that your thoughts become chains of thoughts. Get a determined mind.

Observe

Observe

... the intersection

For a minute.

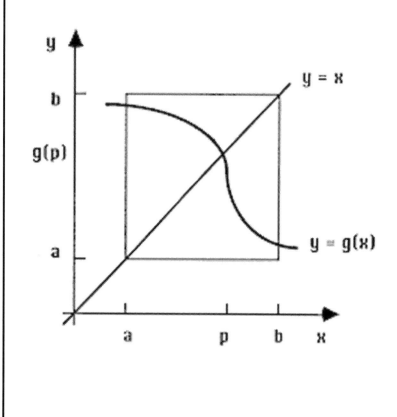

Observe

... the soup

Count all the numbers 4.

```
5 R 4 T 6 F 5 D 4 E 6 R 5 4 T 6 6 E 5 R 4 T
6 R 5 E 4 R 6 T 5 E 4 R T E 6 R 5 4 T 6 I F
A 5 F F 4 F 6 A 5 S 4 F 6 A 5 S 4 Q W E 5 R
4 T 6 Q 5 W 4 R 6 Q 5 W E 4 R 6 Q 5 W I
R Q 3 W 2 E I R Q 3 W 2 I R Q 3 2 W I 5
I T A 5 4 S 6 F 5 A 4 F I A 3 B A 3 B A B 4
C 4 D 5 E F 4 G 6 5 H 4 Y 4 J U 6 5 I O 4 P
6 L I O 5 I U 6 5 Q 5 E 4 R T 4 U 5 I 4 O 4
K 4 J 4 Y U 4 O 4 L 5 I 4 O 5 L 4 K P 4 4 O
5 I 3 O 2 I Ñ 3 K 4 L 4 A 5 S 4 I F D E 5 R
4 F I B I C 5 D E 5 R 4 F 4 E 5 R 4 A 6 S 5
E 4 R 6 E 5 R I F 3 A 2 S I F 3 A 2 I F 3 A
2 Q 4 W 5 E 4 R 6 T 5 R 4 T 4 Y 4 U 5 I 4
O 4 L 4 K 4 J 2 M I N H 2 Y 4 J 4 U 5 I 4 O
4 L I K 3 K 5 K 4 L 6 Y 5 U L 4 Y 9 U 8 I 7
O A 5 5 D 7 4 F 4 E 6 R 5 T 8 G 7 R E 5 R
```

Observe

... the map

For 2 minutes.

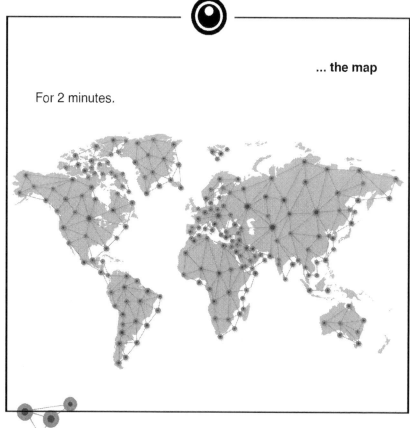

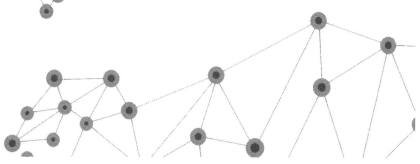

Observe

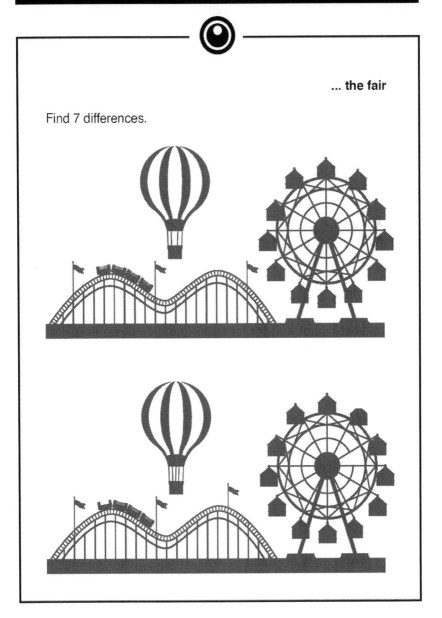

... the fair

Find 7 differences.

Observe

... the clouds

For 2 minutes.

... the numbers

Count aloud or in a low voice.

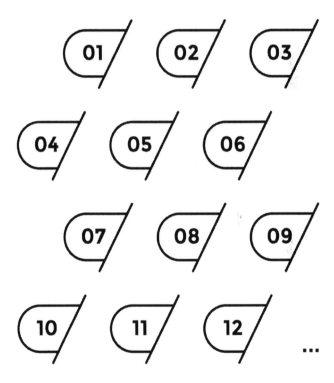

Observe

... the figure

In each row, find the number of the first column.

91348	91358	92348	74625	91348
12712	12212	12712	12812	74512
32684	32644	31684	47512	32684
29435	29445	29434	29435	29935
25755	35770	25755	25760	36765
37102	37112	37102	37002	37202
55055	53035	65056	55055	31203
92274	92274	82274	82273	82277
82325	82545	82735	82325	83325

Observe

.... the alphabet

Spell your name visually.
Repeat as many times as you need.

Observe

... the surround sound

Listen and name all the sounds that you can hear right now surrounding you.

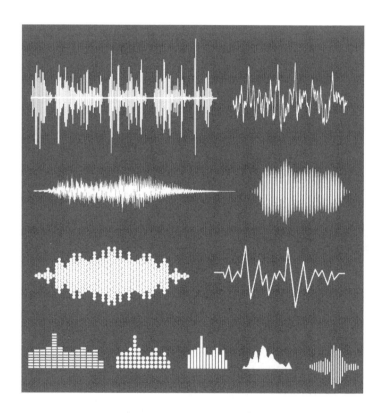

...DO!!

... the surround smell

What is it that you smell?

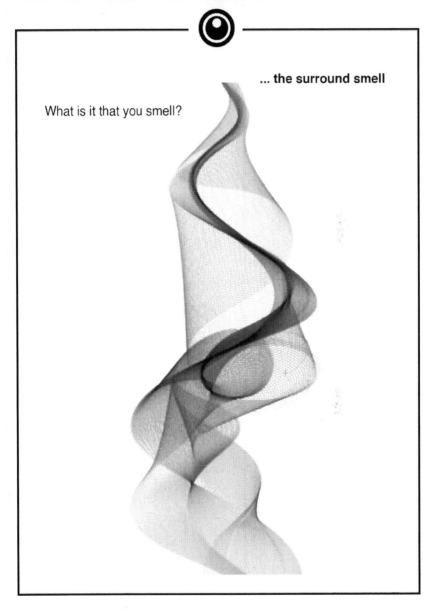

Observe

... the surrounding space

For 5 minutes.
Floors, walls, ceilings, lights, objects, colors, shapes, textures...

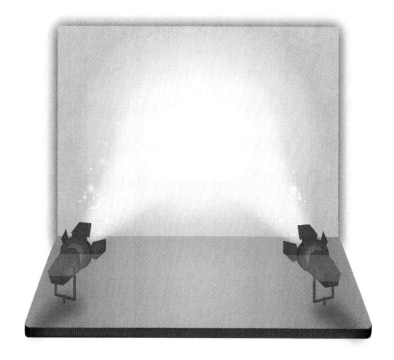

...DO‼

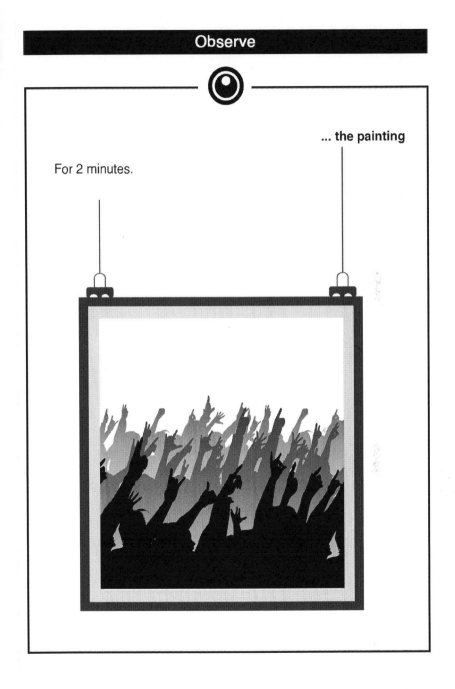

Observe

... the painting

For 2 minutes.

Observe

... your heart rate

Put you index and middle fingers on one side of your neck and feel the LIFE.

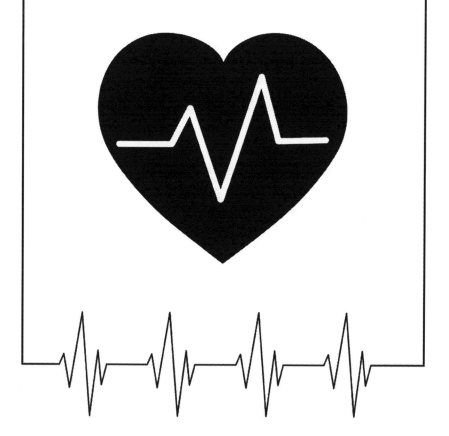

...DO!!

... your hands

For 2 minutes.

pfff...

 **· Draw**

... freely. Stimulate the right hemisphere of your brain (the creative one) and express yourself.

Draw

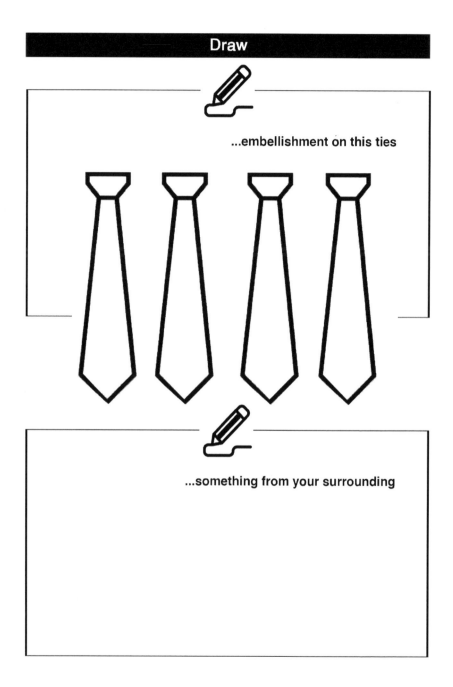

...embellishment on this ties

...something from your surrounding

...DO!!

...a postcard to you

Draw

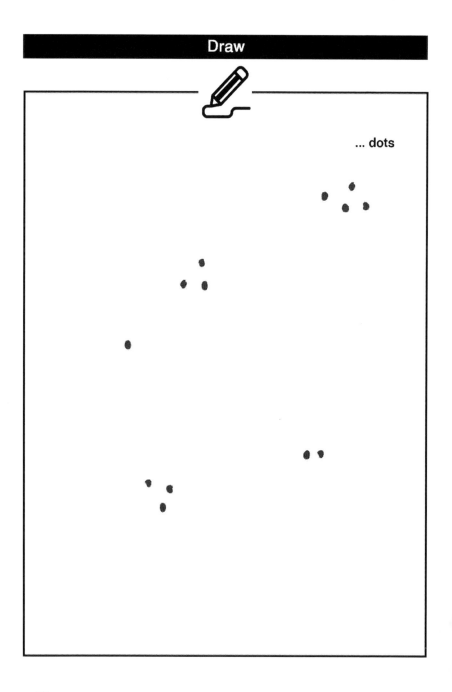

... dots

...DO‼

Draw

... faces

pfff...

Draw

... doodles

Draw

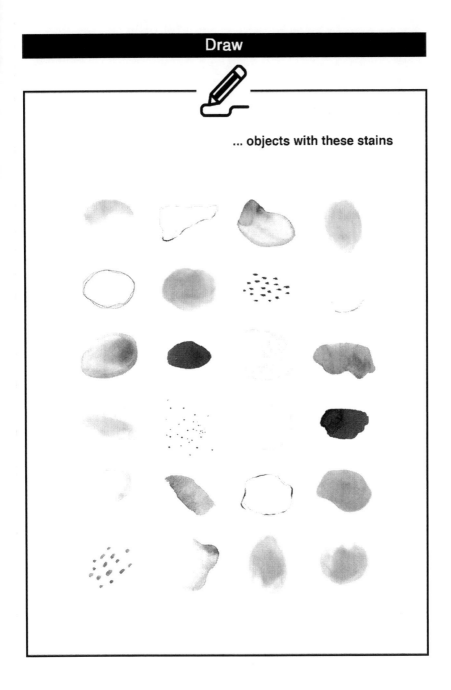

... objects with these stains

Draw

... geometrically shaped animals

Draw

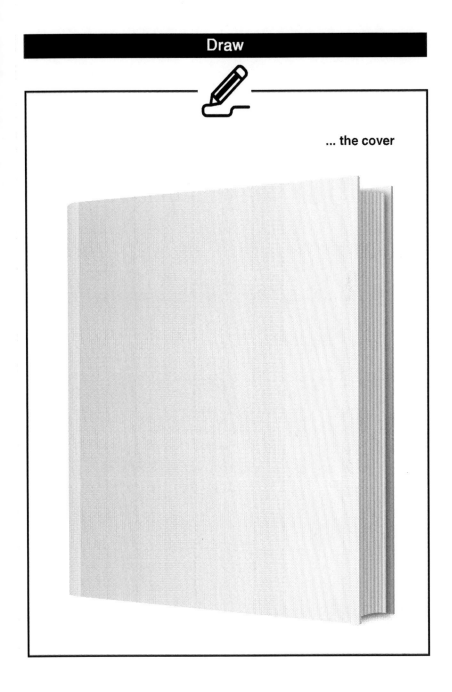

... the cover

Draw

... a natural landscape

...DO‼

Draw

... anything

pfff...

 · Imagine

... in great detail. Develop your mind and enjoy the experiences.

Imagine

**...you put on some green lenses sunglasses,
go for a walk.**

Close your eyes for some minutes and enjoy.

...DO!!

Imagine

**...you are in the middle of a forest,
lie down.**

Close your eyes for some minutes and enjoy.

...a panda bear gives you a hug.

Close your eyes for some minutes and enjoy.

Imagine

**...a long carpet that tickles,
walk barefoot on it.**

Close your eyes for some minutes and enjoy.

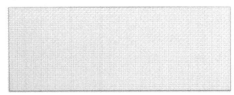

Imagine

**...your favorite song is playing on the radio,
turn up the volume and sing.**

Close your eyes for some minutes and enjoy.

Imagine

**... you are a "salty" alien and everything tastes like salt,
try tasting chocolate.**

Close your eyes for some minutes and enjoy.

Imagine

**...you are granted a wish,
ask for it.**

Close your eyes for some minutes and enjoy.

Imagine

**...you have so much energy you can turn on a bulb,
get a fair started.**

Close your eyes for some minutes and enjoy.

Imagine

...you have some "damp earth" scented spray, use it.

Close your eyes for some minutes and enjoy.

....you have a super power, use it.

Close your eyes for some minutes and enjoy.

pfff...

...DO‼

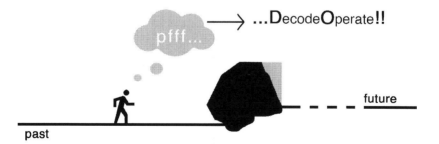

...DecodeOperate‼

future

past

pfff...

...DO!!

...DecodeOperate!!

According the Cambridge Dictionary of English, "DO" means "to perform, take part in, or achieve something."

You have recovered the control of your attention to here and now. It is the moment to ...DO!!! (Decode and Operate) from a more rational, logical and balanced perspective.

pfff...

 # Decode

...the situation that is causing you stress. Discover the direct connection between your thought and you behavior.

Identify the sources causing you stress.

My stress

SITUATION	THOUGHTS

Describe it —○ What did I think?

—○

—○

...DO!!

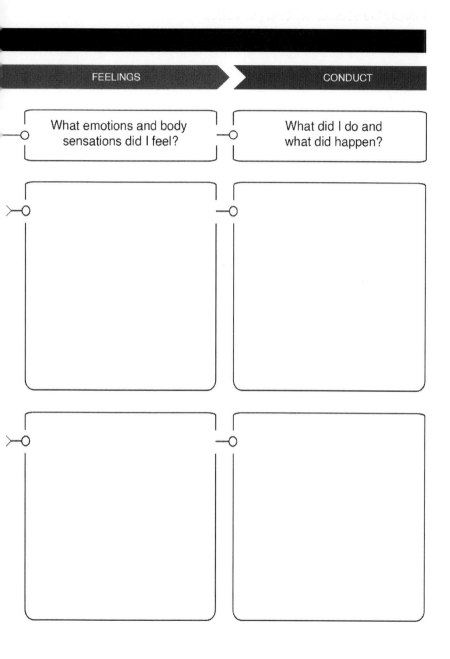

pfff...

My stress

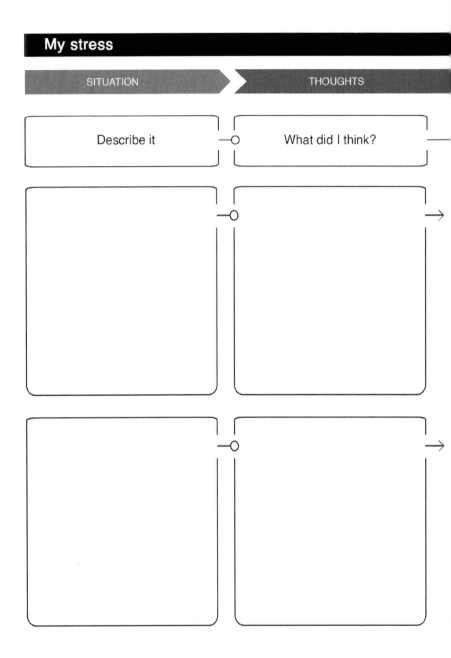

SITUATION

THOUGHTS

Describe it

What did I think?

...DO!!

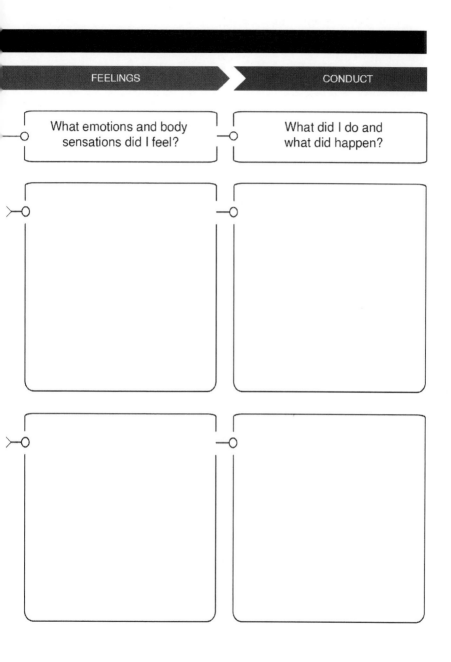

Choose the one that stresses you the most.

The situation

Describe it

Draw it

...DO‼

What did I think?

What are the odds of being understanding the situation properly?

What is the evidence in favor of that thought?

Cognitive DISTORTIONS

They are wrong ways of processing information. They are those automatic thoughts that twist reality (hide it, ignore it, guess it...).

• **Mind reading (arbitrary inference):** when we assume we know what others are thinking and feeling, as well as their intentions of their acts.

• **Filtering (selective abstraction):** when we just take one part of a situation.

• **Polarized Thinking (or "Black and White" Thinking):** when we think in extremes, good-bad, black-white,...

• **Overgeneralization:** when we think that a specific situation will always happen in a certain way.

• **Labeling:** When we describe ourselves or other people in an automatic negative way.

• **Personalization:** when we think we are the cause of everything and that everything that happens is exclusively up to us.

• **Always Being Right:** when we need to be right and we think our opinions and actions are th right ones.

• **Should Statements:** when we think "I should do that" or "I would have to do that" ignoring any other options.

• **Emotional Reasoning:** when whatever we are feeling is believed to be true.

• **Magnification:** when we exaggerate the negative aspects of a situation.

• **Minimization:** when we lessen the positive aspects of a situation.

...DO!!

Identify the distortions of your thinking.

My perception

My thinking

1. Mind reading. Yes/No
2. Filtering. Yes/No
3. Polarized Thinking. Yes/No
4. Overgeneralization. Yes/No
5. Labeling. Yes/No
6. Personalization. Yes/No
7. Always Being Right. Yes/No
8. Should Statements. Yes/No
9. Emotional Reasoning. Yes/No
10. Magnification. Yes/No
11. Minimization. Yes/No

Copy the definition of the distortions that are affirmative for you.

pfff...

...DO‼

 # Operate

...to change your perspective. Overcome your stress.

The situation (describe it objectively)

Now you have to explain it to:

... a friend. What does he/she think?

... a relative. What does he/she think?

... a neighbor. What does he/she think?

...DO!!

... a 5-year-old kid. What does he think?

... a 70-year-old woman. What does she think?

... a man from the USA. What does he think?

██████████████████████████████████

... a millionaire. What does she think?

... a blind person. What does he think?

... a pilot. What does he think?

... a singer. What does she think?

... a sick person. What does he think?

...DO !!

... a pregnant woman. What does she think?

... a prisoner. What does he think?

... a judge. What does she think?

... a boxer. What does he think?

... a widower. What does he think?

pfff...

... etc ...

¡There are as many ways of thinking as people!

...DO!!

Now, read your values and consider your thoughts again.
Define your course of action.

Re-think

The situation

What are you going to do and when?

Review it and keep going on until you overcome your stress.

Step by step

What did you do? ...and, how are you feeling?

What are you going to do and when?

...DO!!

What did you do? ...and, how are you feeling?

What are you going to do and when?

Step by step

What did you do? …and, how are you feeling?

What are you going to do and when?

...DO‼

What did you do? ...and, how are you feeling?

What are you going to do and when?

pfff...

Step by step

What did you do? ...and, how are you feeling?

What are you going to do and when?

...DO!!

What did you do? ...and, how are you feeling?

What are you going to do and when?

pfff...

...DO!!

We are thankful

... for the wonderful miracle of BEING ALIVE.

pfff...

...DO!!

We live as if we are going to live forever, leaving happiness for a future to come. I'll be happy when that happens, or when I have this or that... But happiness is here and now.

YOU'RE ALIVE !!

Life is a gist and we must be thankful for that.

Even though the situation you are going through is hard, you are able to overcome it. In the future, you will be thankful because you learned this lesson, and you will be stronger.

Everything is a matter of perspective and attitude.

Remember
Life is given to us, but we don't know how much time left we have.

Start by being thankful to your body, your family, your friends, your things, for your food, your house, your experiences, your places, your achievements, etc...

... I am thankful to you:

Thank you so, so, so much for existing.

I am thankful

1. _____

2. _____

3. _____

4. _____

5. _____

6. _____

7. _____

8. _____

9. _____

10. _____

I am thankful

11. _____

12. _____

13. _____

14. _____

15. _____

16. _____

17. _____

18. _____

19. _____

20. _____

pfff...

I am thankful

21. _____

22. _____

23. _____

24. _____

25. _____

26. _____

27. _____

28. _____

29. _____

30. _____

...DO!!

31. _____

32. _____

33. _____

34. _____

35. _____

36. _____

37. _____

38. _____

39. _____

40. _____

I am thankful

41. _____

42. _____

43. _____

44. _____

45. _____

46. _____

47. _____

48. _____

49. _____

50. _____

I am thankful

51. _____

52. _____

53. _____

54. _____

55. _____

56. _____

57. _____

58. _____

59. _____

60. _____

I am thankful

61. _____

62. _____

63. _____

64. _____

65. _____

66. _____

67. _____

68. _____

69. _____

70. _____

...DO‼

I am thankful

71. _____

72. _____

73. _____

74. _____

75. _____

76. _____

77. _____

78. _____

79. _____

80. _____

pfff...

Blank pages

... to be FREE.

The real key of life is not what happens to us,
but the way we respond to it.

There is a personal space of freedom between the things
we receive from the world and the way we respond to those things:
the freedom to choose.

SELF-BEING

pfff...

...DO!!

pfff...

...DO!!

pfff…

...DO!!

pfff...

...DO!!

pfff...

...DO!!

Printed in Poland
by Amazon Fulfillment
Poland Sp. z o.o., Wrocław

66230972R00078